D0495431

Questions in
Standard Grade
Business Management

Text copyright © 1999 Margo Barr
Design and layout copyright © 1999 Leckie & Leckie Ltd
Cover image © SCIENCE PHOTO LIBRARY

1st edition (reprinted 2006)

ISBN 1-898890-56-0
ISBN-13 978-1-898890-56-0

Published by
Leckie & Leckie Ltd, 3rd floor, 4 Queen Street, Edinburgh, EH2 1JE
Tel: 0131 220 6831 Fax: 0131 225 9987
enquiries@leckieandleckie.co.uk   www.leckieandleckie.co.uk

Edited by
John McDonald

Special thanks to
Latte Goldstein (cover design)

Leckie & Leckie Ltd is a division of Huveaux plc.

Margo Barr

CONTENTS

INTRODUCTION

The questions in this book will help you to prepare for your Standard Grade Business Management exam.

- The Standard Grade Business Management course covers four areas:

  1. What is business?

  2. How do businesses develop and perform?

  3. What resources do businesses use?

  4. How are businesses managed?

  The questions in this book are set out in this order and are further divided into subunits as shown on the Contents page.

- There are three assessable elements in the Standard Grade Business Management course. These are:

  · Knowledge and Understanding (KU)

  · Decision-making (DM)

  · Practical Abilities (PA)

  The questions in this book cover KU and DM at Foundation, General and Credit Level.

- Answers are provided in the pull-out centre section.

- To help you in your revision, the answer section shows you which questions are Foundation Level, which are General Level and which are Credit Level using the following system:

Answers to Foundation Level questions are printed on a plain background (like this).
Answers to General Level questions are printed on a hatched background (like this).
Answers to Credit Level questions are printed on a shaded background (like this).

  In some questions, the content of the question may be Foundation Level, but the language that is used or the level of difficulty is General Level. The question then becomes a General Level question. This will also happen in the exam.

  You should attempt all the questions. Check with your teacher, however, about which Levels you are sitting in the exam.

  Question 24 is very difficult and questions in the exam are unlikely to be of this calibre. However, it will stretch you before the exam, and can also be used after the exam as an introduction to Higher work. It is also a good teacher-led question for the whole class to cover together.

- Spend time revising each topic and then try the questions on that topic. To help you with your revision, we recommend that you obtain a copy of Leckie & Leckie's other Business Management book, *Standard Grade Business Management Course Notes*, from your school, college or bookstore.

  At the foot of every page of questions you will find references to Leckie & Leckie's *Standard Grade Business Management Course Notes*. Look up these pages for help with answering the questions.

- Use a jotter or paper for your answers.
  To answer some questions you will need a calculator, and a ruler for drawing tables.

EXAM PREPARATION

As stated in the introduction, the Standard Grade Business Management exam has three assessable elements. Two of these – Knowledge and Understanding and Decision-making – are directly covered by this book. These are assessed by **one** written exam at **each** level, i.e. F, G or C level.

1. **Checklist**
    *   Tick the question checklist at the end of the answer section when you complete each question.
    *   The questions do not need to be tackled in the order given here.
    *   Your checklist will remind you of the sections you have covered.

2. **Notes and Answers**
    *   The core information needed to answer the questions in this book is found in Leckie & Leckie's *Standard Grade Business Management Course Notes*.
    *   Although it is tempting to look at the answers first, they will not help you learn much if you do it all the time!
    *   Learn about each subunit, then try the questions, then check the answers.
    *   Alter your answer as appropriate – do not leave any wrong answer unchanged.

3. **Practical Abilities**
    *   The third assessable element – Practical Abilities – is internally assessed.
    *   It involves the use of a business simulation on a CD-ROM.
    *   You will complete this as part of your course – it is not a written exam.
    *   KU and DM skills will be required before you can successfully carry out the CD-ROM tasks.

    Example:
    While using the CD-ROM, you may be required to decide on the location of a business. To do this you will need knowledge about location of industry. This is covered in section 3.1 in both *Standard Grade Business Management Course Notes* and in *Questions in Standard Grade Business Management*.

NOTE TO TEACHERS

This book was conceived and written when the Standard Grade Business Management course was in the pilot stage, and before the first Standard Grade Business Management exam was produced.

It is proposed that the book will be revised, if necessary, once the course has run for a longer period. Your comments will be gratefully received.

As stated in the introduction, the book covers the KU and DM assessable elements. These have not been specified exactly at this stage, but as a guide, it is suggested that the following questions could be used as preparation for the DM elements:

Q61 (c); (e)(ii)	Q20 (c)(ii); (d)
Q62 (b)	Q24 (a); (c)
Q65 (b); (c)(i),(ii) & (iii)	Q27 (e)
Q67 (b); (c)(ii); (d)(ii) & (iii)	Q29
Q72 (b)	Q55 (b)(i) & (ii)
Q73 (c)	Q58
Q75 (b)	

This list is given as a rough guide only.

Margo Barr

Margo Barr

1 WHAT IS BUSINESS?

1.1 WHAT DO BUSINESSES DO?

1. (a) From the pictures below, copy and complete the following table, by writing each item into the correct column.

Goods	Services

Computers   Wine   Fire Brigade   Fishing

Light bulbs   Bus ride   University education   Hammer

(b) Which two pictures in part (a) represent businesses in the **public sector**?

(c) Name one difference between the private and public sectors of industry.

(d) Look again at the pictures in part (a). Each of them has been produced in, or is an example of, the primary, secondary and tertiary sectors of industry. Copy and complete the table below, showing which column each item should go into.

Sectors of Industry		
Primary	Secondary	Tertiary

1. (e) What is the difference between needs and wants?

   (f) Describe what is meant by the following terms:
       (i) production
       (ii) consumption

2. (a) What is the term for a business owned by one person?

   (b) What is the usual maximum number of partners in a partnership?

   (c) Small businesses usually employ less than ___ people. What is the missing figure?

   (d) Name two differences between small and large businesses.

   (e) What type of organisation is described below?
       'Its main aim is to care for those in need of help, and to do so it asks for donations from the public and raises funds in other ways. It does not aim to make a profit.'

   (f) Copy out the following table.

Private Sector	Public Sector	Voluntary Sector
Bicycle Shop		

   Put the businesses shown below into the correct columns of the above table. The first one has been done for you.

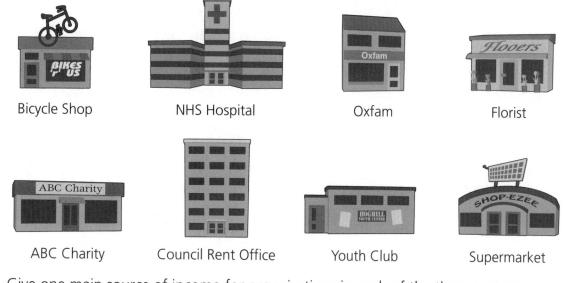

Bicycle Shop   NHS Hospital   Oxfam   Florist

ABC Charity   Council Rent Office   Youth Club   Supermarket

   (g) Give one main source of income for organisations in each of the three sectors shown in part (f), i.e. private, public and voluntary.

3. (a) Write a paragraph explaining what is meant by the term 'creating wealth'.

   (b) Name three different types of businesses and/or producers which might be involved from the raw material stage to the final production of the table shown here.

   (c) State how wealth might be created between each of the processes which you named in part (b).

   (d) The table is finally put up for sale in a large furniture store which is owned by shareholders and aims to maximise profit. The store employs between 50 and 250 people.
      (i) From the choices given below, state which **two** sectors of business the store comes into.

      | primary sector | secondary sector | tertiary sector |
      | private sector | public sector | voluntary sector |

      (ii) Is the store an example of a small, medium or large business? Give a reason for your answer.

1.2 WHY DO BUSINESSES EXIST?

4. Match the following terms A–D with the correct descriptions 1–4 in the box below.

Terms	Descriptions
A Enterprise	1 When goods are sold for a higher price than they cost
B Profit	2 Developing a new idea
C Charity	3 A state school is an example of this
D Public Service	4 Oxfam is an example of this

A	B	C	D

5. (a) To start up a business requires (among other things) 'enterprise'. What is meant by this term?

   (b) What is the name given to someone who has 'enterprise'? Give two examples of this type of person, i.e. name two real people.

   (c) Name three risks which a person starting a new business might face during the first year of business.

   (d) Business can be divided into the private sector, public sector or voluntary sector.
      (i) Marks & Spencer is in the private sector. Give another example of a private sector organisation.

5. (d) (ii) Name **one** organisation in each of the other two sectors, i.e. public and voluntary.
   (iii) Each of the organisations you named in parts (i) and (ii) have different aims. State what you think the **main** aim of **each** one of the three organisations is likely to be.
   (iv) Give examples of two stakeholders in each organisation named in parts (i) and (ii). State in each case, what **their** main interest in the organisation might be.

6. (a) Copy out the table below, and complete the 'Main Aim' column using one of the following terms: **profit, charity, public service**. Each term can be used more than once. The first one has been completed for you.

Name of Organisation	Main Aim
B & Q	profit
Oxfam	
Grampian Police	
Tesco	
Save the Children	
Poppies Garden Centre	
NHS	

   (b) Businesses can bring social costs and benefits to their local communities. They can also bring economic costs and benefits.
   (i) What is the difference between social costs and social benefits? Give two examples of each.
   (ii) What is the difference between economic costs and economic benefits? Give two examples of each.

7. The Blue Sox Football Club plc is a large, profit-making organisation. Copy and complete the table below, listing three stakeholders and their possible interests in the club. An example is given to help you.

Stakeholders	Possible Interest
Fans	Attending/watching matches. Some will also be shareholders who are interested in the profits too.

1.3 HOW ARE BUSINESSES ORGANISED?

8. (a) The diagrams below demonstrate two organisation structures. What are they called?

   (i)   (ii)

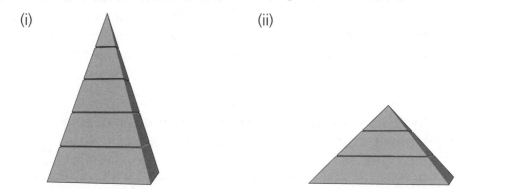

   (b) (i) What are the main differences between the two structures?
       (ii) Which one represents a more traditional approach to business organisation?

   (c) What is meant by the term 'span of control'? Use diagrams to illustrate your answer.

   (d) The Administration and Human Resources Departments have 'functional relationships' with other departments in an organisation.
       (i) What is a 'functional relationship'?
       (ii) Name two services which:
           A the Administration Department gives to other departments
           B the Human Resources Department gives to other departments.

   (e) Give a definition of both:
       (i) authority
       (ii) responsibility
       showing clearly the difference between the two.

   (f) Draw a simple diagram to illustrate line relationships, and state what they mean.

2 HOW DO BUSINESSES DEVELOP AND PERFORM?

2.1 HOW DO BUSINESSES START?

9.

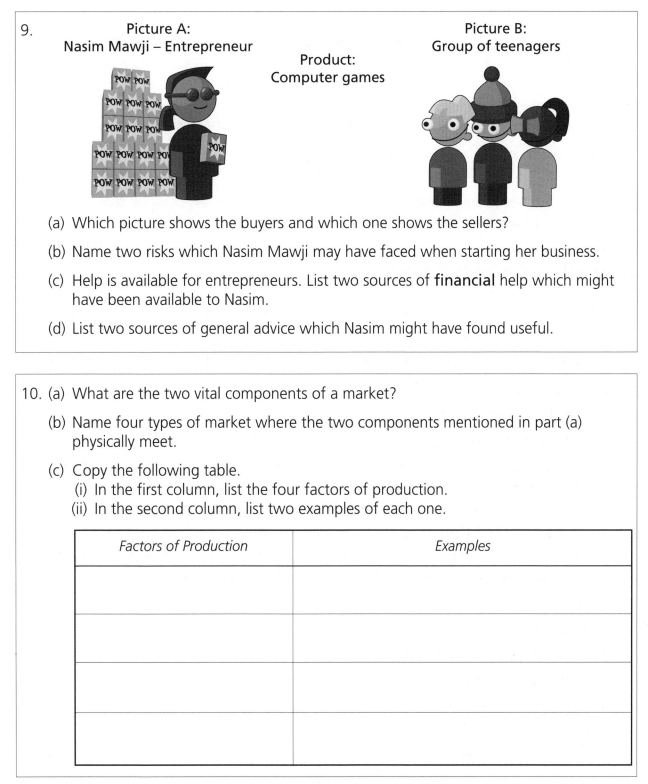

Picture A:
Nasim Mawji – Entrepreneur

Product:
Computer games

Picture B:
Group of teenagers

(a) Which picture shows the buyers and which one shows the sellers?

(b) Name two risks which Nasim Mawji may have faced when starting her business.

(c) Help is available for entrepreneurs. List two sources of **financial** help which might have been available to Nasim.

(d) List two sources of general advice which Nasim might have found useful.

10. (a) What are the two vital components of a market?

(b) Name four types of market where the two components mentioned in part (a) physically meet.

(c) Copy the following table.
   (i) In the first column, list the four factors of production.
   (ii) In the second column, list two examples of each one.

Factors of Production	Examples

11. Before a business starts up, it is expected that the owners will know something about the market for their product or service.

   (a) Name the two main ways of researching the market.

   (b) Define each term given in your answer to part (a). Show clearly the difference between them, giving examples of each.

   (c) Name two ways in which some of the risks which a new business faces can be avoided.

12. (a) Write a sentence, or very short paragraph, stating what a Business Plan is.

   (b) (i) Name **one** important external agency which is likely to see this Plan.
      (ii) What is the likely purpose of showing the Business Plan to this agency?

   (c) The Business Plan contains essential information. Name and describe **five** main areas covered by a good Business Plan.

2.2 HOW DO BUSINESSES GROW?

13. Match the following descriptions A–E with the terms 1–5 according to which ones you think are most correct. Each term (1–5) can only be used once.

   Copy and complete the box shown at the end of the question.

   ### Descriptions

   A Two businesses (usually of similar size) agree to join together.

   B One business takes over another. Usually the one doing this is the larger of the two.

   C Each of the businesses joining together produces the same product and is at the same stage of production.

   D Businesses at different stages of production join together. The business at the beginning of the chain takes over the next link, and so on.

   E Businesses at different stages of production join together. The business at the end of the chain takes over the business at the stage before it, and so on.

   ### Terms

   1 Takeover

   2 Forward vertical integration

   3 Horizontal integration

   4 Backward vertical integration

   5 Merger

A	B	C	D	E

14. Some businesses diversify into producing several very different products and services at the same time.

    (a) Give one advantage of this to a business.

    (b) Name two methods by which businesses can diversify.

15. (a) Although research and development cost money, why are many businesses still prepared to pay for them?

    (b) Many businesses carry out market research and product research. Briefly describe what is meant by each of these terms.

    (c) Once research is carried out, development of a product or service takes place. Name two steps which may take place in the development of a new rollercoaster in a theme park.

16. (a) Give four reasons why a business might want to grow.

    (b) As a business grows it will probably achieve **economies of scale**. Explain the term 'economies of scale'.

    (c) (i) What is the difference between external and internal economies of scale?
        (ii) Give two examples of each.

    (d) Give two reasons why one business might decide to take over another.

17. One way to keep ahead of competitors is to be prepared to introduce **innovations.**

    (a) Explain the term 'innovation'.

    (b) How can innovation help a company to keep ahead of its competitors?

    (c) Why is research and development an important element in achieving innovation?

2.3 HOW DO BUSINESSES SURVIVE?

18. Planning is important in any business. A theme park decides to develop a new water feature. This will be a 'river adventure' including whirlpools, rapids and rocks which boats must navigate.

    Copy and complete the following table, listing three other planning questions which the planners should consider. One question has been done to help you.

	Planning Questions
1	What will it cost to build?
2	
3	
4	

19.

	Jan	Feb	Mar	Apr
	£000	£000	£000	£000
Income	10	13	15	10
Costs	15	15	15	15

    (a) In which month are costs covered in this business?

    (b) From the words in bold below, choose the correct word which is missing from the following sentence:

    The above extract is a **forecast**. It is, therefore, a form of _____ .

        production   planning   marketing   information technology

    (c) The above extract comes from a document which predicts future receipts and payments of cash. What is the name given to this document?

    (d) In the months when costs are **not** covered, how will the business obtain money to pay for them? Name two methods of obtaining the necessary funds.

    (e) How will the information in this document help the business's owners to control the business's money for the next four months?

20.

Bandbox Ltd		
	Year 1	Year 2
	£000	£000
Sales turnover	250	300
less Cost of sales	(100)	(120)
Gross Profit	**150**	**180**
less Expenses	(50)	(60)
Net Profit	£____	£____

(a) What is the name of this final account?

(b) Calculate net profit for year 1 and year 2.

(c) (i) Calculate the net profit-to-sales ratio for both years, showing your working clearly.

(ii) Explain what has happened to the net profit-to-sales ratio between the two years. Give one possible reason for this, stating whether it is a good or bad indicator for the business.

(d) When the company compares its final accounts with that of a rival business, Hatbox, it discovers the following information for year 2:

	Hatbox Ltd	Bandbox Ltd
	£000	£000
Sales turnover	320	300
less Cost of sales	(211)	(120)
Gross Profit	**109**	**180**
less Expenses	(80)	(60)
Net Profit	**29**	**120**
Capital employed	120	140

Which one of the two companies do you think is the better managed? Give reasons for your answer, using ratios where appropriate.

21. Properly used, ratios tell observers about the three main areas of a business's finances: profitability, liquidity and asset usage.
Name, and give formulae for, two ratios which are calculated for profitability and two which are calculated for liquidity.

2.4 WHY DO BUSINESSES FAIL?

22. Pete's Clothing Store has closed down. In the next street, the New Stylez shop attracts buyers looking for designer clothing. Clothes-R-Us sells fashionable clothes at low prices. Pete's shop had neither the advantage of selling exclusive clothes like New Stylez, nor up-to-date fashions like Clothes-R-Us.

Each picture A–D represents a different reason for Pete's failure. From the list below, match a reason to each picture listed in the table. Copy and complete the table. Note that two reasons should be left out.

Reasons

1 Competition from this designer shop was too fierce.

2 There were no parking facilities.

3 Pete's was behind the times compared to this business.

4 Recession in the economy

5 Cash flow problems

6 There was a labour shortage.

Picture	Reasons
A New Stylez	
B Clothes-R-Us	
C Newspaper Headline	
D Pete's Accounts	

23. Competition can have an important part to play in a business's failure. The following are practised by the **competitors** of Airjet Limited – a small company which is struggling:

Terms

A Destroyer pricing

C Better quality services and lower prices

B Restrictive practices

D Newer ideas

Match these terms A–D with the correct descriptions 1–4 shown below. Copy and complete the box shown at the end of this question. Use each description only **once**.

Descriptions

1 This involves illegal agreements between businesses to cut down competition.

2 This involves selling at very low prices to cause the failure of competitors.

3 Airjet is not moving with the times compared with some of its competitors.

4 This is likely to increase demand for competitors' products because of quality, etc.

A	B	C	D

24. The Brent Hotel is a medium-sized, family-run hotel which has been operating for thirty years. Its main competitors are the nearby Royal Hotel and the Burns Hotel. Both of these hotels are thriving while the Brent is struggling.

Of the three hotels, the Brent is the most run-down. The decor in the public rooms has seen better days and the huge, weed-infested grounds are less attractive than the other two. Better parking facilities are required.

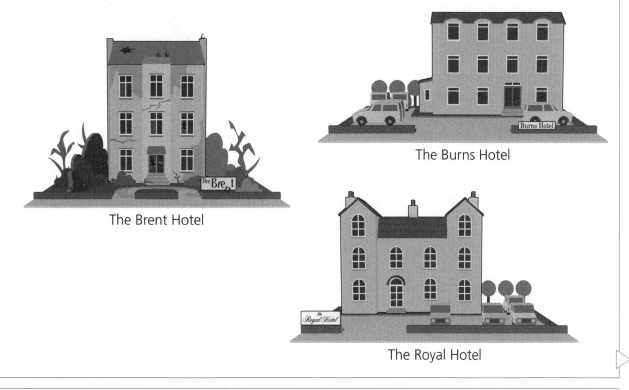

The Burns Hotel

The Brent Hotel

The Royal Hotel

24. (cont.) The management of the Royal and the Burns Hotels (unlike the Brent) have recognised the importance of providing cut-price packages at weekends when business people do not use the hotels. These reduced rates encourage families and couples at a time when hotels would be lying empty – like the Brent is! The Brent charges the same rates seven days a week, and their weekend rates are much higher than the Royal or the Burns. Their rates for single rooms are also much higher than the other two hotels. The Royal and the Burns have realised that these two areas of pricing have become very important selling points in recent years. Many single travellers now demand better rates, so the Brent loses their custom.

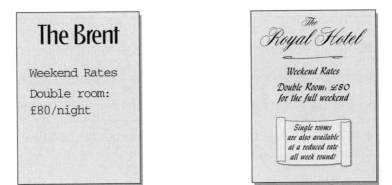

The Brent does not offer conference facilities for business clients, unlike the Royal and the Burns which find these very popular services extremely profitable. It does not have a computer system for bookings, appointments and accounts. The other two hotels do. At the Brent, all of these operations are handwritten by staff and this causes errors, delays and cancelled bookings.

The Brent's profits fell by £30,000 this year. Also, despite having the same number of rooms as the Royal and the Burns Hotels, booking and profits were only one-third of those gained by the other two hotels. The Brent is suffering from poor resource management, and if improvements are not made, the Brent Hotel might have to close within a year.

(a) One of the problems for the Brent Hotel is its failure to respond to change. Name three instances of this and state why each of these has affected the hotel's profitability.

(b) (i) What is meant by the term 'poor resource management'?
    (ii) Give three examples of this in the Brent Hotel. Use different examples from part (a) if possible.

(c) (i) Suggest four improvements which the hotel could make to its current practices.
    (ii) Suggest two ways in which the hotel could promote these improvements to the public.

2.5 WHAT IS A SUCCESSFUL BUSINESS?

25. Success means different things to different organisations.

    (a) Give one example of an organisation in each sector listed below. An example has been given for the first one. Provide another example for this sector.

        • public sector: e.g. *fire service*, _____

        • private sector: e.g. _____

        • voluntary sector: e.g. _____

    (b) (i) For each of the organisations listed in part (a), give two ways in which each one measures success.
        (ii) Are the measures of success different in each sector?
        (iii) If the answer to part (ii) is yes, give reasons for this.

26.

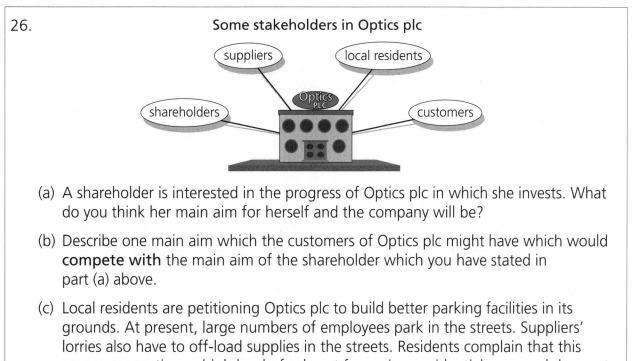

Some stakeholders in Optics plc

    (a) A shareholder is interested in the progress of Optics plc in which she invests. What do you think her main aim for herself and the company will be?

    (b) Describe one main aim which the customers of Optics plc might have which would **compete with** the main aim of the shareholder which you have stated in part (a) above.

    (c) Local residents are petitioning Optics plc to build better parking facilities in its grounds. At present, large numbers of employees park in the streets. Suppliers' lorries also have to off-load supplies in the streets. Residents complain that this causes congestion, a high level of exhaust fumes in a residential area, and danger to local children crossing streets. Residents also have difficulty in parking outside their own homes. If Optics plc agrees to their demands, the residents will benefit but other stakeholders might not.
        (i) State which stakeholders shown in the diagram might not benefit from this action in the short term. Give reasons.
        (ii) What benefits might some, or all, of the stakeholders gain in the long term as a result of this action?
        (iii) If the company does not take action, the residents will continue to experience the social costs of having Optics plc in their neighbourhood. State what these social costs are.
        (iv) Four types of stakeholders are shown in the diagram. Name three other groups of people who will have a stake in Optics plc, and explain what their interests are likely to be (in general).

3 WHAT RESOURCES DO BUSINESSES USE?

3.1 WHY DO BUSINESSES LOCATE WHERE THEY DO?

27.

(a) Look at the picture above. List three things which might have encouraged Donny to open an ice-cream shop there.

(b) Donny needs more money because he wants to extend his premises. Name two possible sources of financial capital which might be available to him.

(c) The government sometimes helps businesses to set up new premises in certain areas. Which areas are likely to receive the most assistance and why?

(d) What kind of assistance does the EU give to help reduce unemployment and factory closures in the UK?

(e) Explain what is meant by the term 'multinational company'. What factors will influence where it locates its business, and what problems is it likely to face once it has located abroad?

---

28. (a) A medium-sized car manufacturing company is about to locate in the north of England. The owners decide to build the factory near a town with high unemployment levels. Name four sources of finance which might be available to the owners for this purpose.

(b) The following factors influenced the owners in deciding where to build the factory.

infrastructure   nearness to market   local raw materials

Explain the meaning of each term and give one example of each, showing how it will be helpful to the factory owners.

---

29. A manufacturer of toys has decided to locate a factory near Aberdeen. About 20% of the toys are exported. The Board of Directors has asked you to write a report advising them on whether this site is suitable.

What information would you need to gather in order to compile an accurate and helpful report?

30. When identifying possible locations for a business, its owners have to consider a number of factors.

The following list shows some of these location factors:

availability of raw materials   availability of land

distance to the market   transport costs

availability of labour   infrastructure

Choose **three** out of these six factors. For each factor chosen, describe the type of business which might find it the most important location factor. 'Availability of raw materials' has been done as an example for you.

Availability of raw materials

Example answer 1: Businesses which depend on bulky raw materials, such as steel production, will find their transport costs are reduced if they locate near to where the raw materials are produced.

Example answer 2: Businesses which depend on processing perishable goods (e.g. vegetables, fruit and fish) will locate near these raw materials.

31.

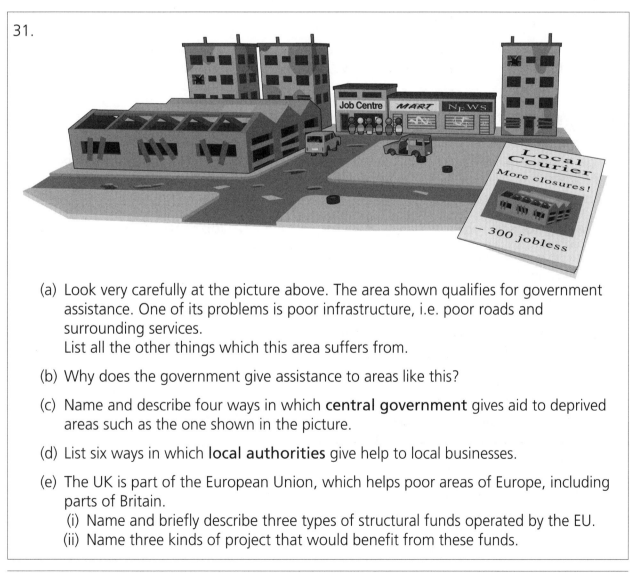

(a) Look very carefully at the picture above. The area shown qualifies for government assistance. One of its problems is poor infrastructure, i.e. poor roads and surrounding services.
List all the other things which this area suffers from.

(b) Why does the government give assistance to areas like this?

(c) Name and describe four ways in which **central government** gives aid to deprived areas such as the one shown in the picture.

(d) List six ways in which **local authorities** give help to local businesses.

(e) The UK is part of the European Union, which helps poor areas of Europe, including parts of Britain.
 (i) Name and briefly describe three types of structural funds operated by the EU.
 (ii) Name three kinds of project that would benefit from these funds.

32. If a business sets up business in an EU country, it will find that the **single market** has many advantages.

   (a) Briefly explain the term **single market**.

   (b) Name and briefly describe three advantages which the single market brings to a business which locates in an EU country.

   (c) Give two disadvantages of the single market.

   (d) Some non-EU companies have set up businesses in EU countries. Name two non-EU countries whose companies have done this.

   (e) What advantages are there for:
      (i) these non-EU companies which set up in the EU
      (ii) the areas in which they set up in business?

33. For some very large businesses such as the producers of Coca-Cola, the market is worldwide. Coca-Cola uses the same advertising and packaging throughout the world.

   (a) What kind of brand is Coca-Cola?

   (b) State what is meant by the 'global market', and give two advantages of this to a business such as Coca-Cola.

   (c) Internationally branded goods are often more popular in countries such as India and China than their local, less expensive, products. Give two reasons for this.

3.2 HOW DO PEOPLE CONTRIBUTE TO BUSINESSES?

34. Four jobs are described in descriptions A–D below. Decide which one you think is temporary, part-time, full-time or permanent. Copy the box shown at the end of the question and match the appropriate numbers (1–4) to the letters.

   Descriptions

   A Julie works every day of the week from approximately 9–5.

   B Ted's job will only last for one year.

   C Shanti's job is likely to continue until he retires unless his firm closes, he is sacked or he is made redundant.

   D Andy works three afternoons a week as a mechanic in his local garage.

   Job Status

   1 Temporary

   2 Part-time

   3 Full-time

   4 Permanent

A	B	C	D

35. The local sports centre has a vacancy. The job entails the supervision and teaching of swimming classes three mornings per week. Travelling to several other sports centres will be necessary at least once a week and occasionally in the evenings. There will be some paperwork and administration involved, and working with other people will occur at regular intervals.

Copy and complete the Person Specification below, ticking which qualities or qualifications you consider:

(a) essential for the job
(b) desirable for the job

Leave blank any qualities or qualifications which you do not think are essential or desirable for this particular job.

Person Specification		
Qualities/Qualifications	Essential	Desirable
Life-saving qualification		
Driving licence		
Honours degree		
Previous experience		
Ability to supervise a team		
Enthusiasm		
Excellent interactive skills (i.e. can get on with people)		
Some clerical skills		
Knowledge of local area		
First aid certificate		
Experience of working with animals		
Punctuality		
Ability to swim		

36. Match the following terms A–D with the correct definitions 1–4. Copy and complete the box at the end of the question. Use each definition only **once**.

Terms

A Manual workers

B White collar workers

C Professionals

D Repetitive tasks

Definitions

1 These workers are skilled labour.

2 These workers are unskilled.

3 These are usually done by blue collar workers.

4 Lawyers and doctors are covered by this term.

A	B	C	D

37. Match the following terms A–C with the correct definitions 1–3. Copy and complete the box at the end of the question. Use each definition only **once**.

Terms

A On-the-job training

B Off-the-job training

C Apprenticeship

Definitions

1 Occurs outside the workplace, at a local college or training centre

2 Mostly occurs in the workplace, but with some external training, e.g. one day a week at college

3 Occurs in the workplace

A	B	C

38. Explain the following terms:

(a) induction training

(b) retraining

(c) upgrading training.

39. Digitz Ltd is a medium-sized business producing components for computers. It has operated a successful formal staff appraisal system for four years.

   (a) Write a paragraph explaining what is meant by staff appraisal, showing clearly the difference between informal and formal appraisal.

   (b) List five features of a successful staff appraisal.

   (c) What are:
       (i) the positive aspects of appraisal
       (ii) the negative aspects of appraisal
       for both managers and staff?

   (d) What is target-setting and why is it important in any staff appraisal system?

40. Businesses can only be successful if the relationship between employees and employers can be clearly defined and understood by both.

   (a) Name five pieces of legislation which affect employees in their place of work.

   (b) (i) When a new employee is taken on, what must he or she be given within thirteen weeks of starting work?
       (ii) State four things which this item should include.

   (c) If the relationship between employers and employees breaks down, industrial action can occur. Name and briefly describe four types of industrial action which can be taken by employees.

   (d) One way of avoiding strained relationships between management and staff is to encourage employee participation. Name and describe two examples of this.

41. In the UK, there has been a major shift in employment from the secondary to the tertiary sector over the last 30–40 years.

   (a) Write a paragraph explaining why this shift has occurred.

   (b) Define the following terms, showing clearly the difference between them:
       (i) casual workers
       (ii) core workers.

   (c) The employment of casual and core workers in a business is a fairly recent trend. Name and describe one other recent employment trend.

3.3 HOW DO BUSINESSES USE INFORMATION?

42.

Information can be transmitted in various ways. Two of these are by **paper** and by **technology**.

(a) Look carefully at the picture of the office. List four examples of **paper** information which are shown there.

(b) Look at the picture again. List three examples of **technological** information shown in the picture.

(c) Information can also be divided into **internal** and **external** information. From the picture of the office:
   (i) list three examples of internal information shown there
   (ii) list four items of information and/or equipment which are examples of contacts with the outside world (i.e. external information).

43. Correct and relevant information is very important to businesses. Customers are vital to profit-making organisations.

(a) Mrs Young phones a furniture removal company for a quote for moving from Leeds to Cardiff. How should this information be given to her? The first answer is given as an example. There are three others.

   (i) *politely*   (ii) _____   (iii) _____   (iv) _____

(b) Explain why the information should be given in the manner described in part (a).

44. The following terms describe software applications which provide information on computers. Match terms A–E with descriptions 1–5. Copy and complete the box at the end of the question. Use each description only **once**.

Terms

A word-processor

B spreadsheet

C database

D graphics

E desktop publishing

Descriptions

1 an electronic filing system containing information such as customer records

2 used for advanced page-layout techniques required in the production of high-quality leaflets, brochures and other printed documents

3 mainly used for recording figures and doing calculations

4 mainly used for producing letters, memos and notices

5 used for the production of charts, graphs and drawings

A	B	C	D	E

45. Businesses must decide what information is relevant to them.

   (a) List four other things which they must consider about the information they receive.

   (b) The points shown in part (a) are the first part of the evaluation process. The second part involves looking at specific items such as **accounts**, **worker performance** and **production**.

   Use each **bold** word above as a heading and, under each heading, list the kinds of information which might be evaluated. The first item in the **accounts** list has been completed for you as an example.

   Accounts
   comparison of profits between years

46. Copy and complete the table below.

(a) In column 2, give **two** types of information which **each** software application can produce and, in column 3, give an example of possible content for each. This can be work which is done within a business itself or is received from outside.

(b) In column 4, show what kind of decision this might lead managers to make. Half of the first one has been done for you as an example. Complete the rest of the table.

Software Application		Work Produced	Possible Content	Decision Made
word-processor	(i)	letter	application for a job	whether or not to grant the applicant an interview
	(ii)			
database	(i)			
	(ii)			
spreadsheet	(i)			
	(ii)			

3.4 HOW DO BUSINESSES OPERATE?

47.

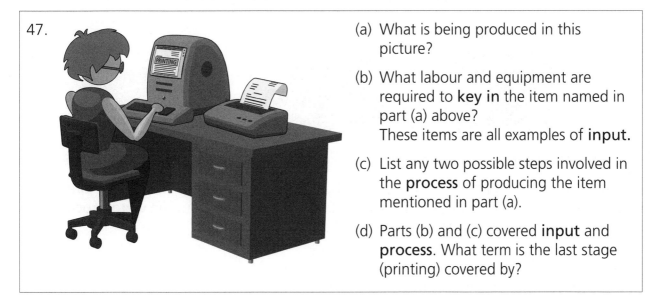

(a) What is being produced in this picture?

(b) What labour and equipment are required to **key in** the item named in part (a) above?
These items are all examples of **input**.

(c) List any two possible steps involved in the **process** of producing the item mentioned in part (a).

(d) Parts (b) and (c) covered **input** and **process**. What term is the last stage (printing) covered by?

---

48. There are several channels of distribution which the factory shown below can use.

One is to open a factory shop and sell directly to customers from there.

List four other ways in which customers can (legally) obtain these bicycles.

---

49. Look at the three pictures below. They are examples of three different methods of production.

A

B

C

State what each method of production is. Your answer should be shown as follows:

A: _____

B: _____

C: _____

50. **Preparing a pot plant for sale in Seedlingz Nursery**

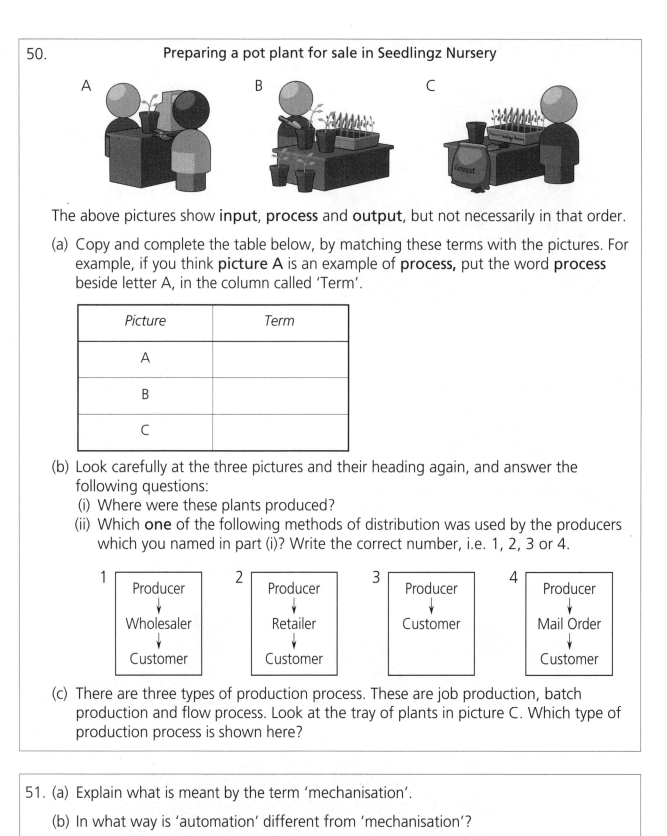

A   B   C

The above pictures show **input**, **process** and **output**, but not necessarily in that order.

(a) Copy and complete the table below, by matching these terms with the pictures. For example, if you think **picture A** is an example of **process,** put the word **process** beside letter A, in the column called 'Term'.

Picture	Term
A	
B	
C	

(b) Look carefully at the three pictures and their heading again, and answer the following questions:
  (i) Where were these plants produced?
  (ii) Which **one** of the following methods of distribution was used by the producers which you named in part (i)? Write the correct number, i.e. 1, 2, 3 or 4.

1
Producer
↓
Wholesaler
↓
Customer

2
Producer
↓
Retailer
↓
Customer

3
Producer
↓
Customer

4
Producer
↓
Mail Order
↓
Customer

(c) There are three types of production process. These are job production, batch production and flow process. Look at the tray of plants in picture C. Which type of production process is shown here?

---

51. (a) Explain what is meant by the term 'mechanisation'.

(b) In what way is 'automation' different from 'mechanisation'?

(c) In manufacturing industry, mechanisation and automation have caused many job losses.
  (i) What kinds of jobs do you think this statement mainly refers to?
  (ii) Give two advantages which automation brings to a manufacturer.
  (iii) Give two examples of banking technology which have reduced the need for bank tellers.

(d) New technology has increased the demand for skilled workers. What are governments and businesses doing to increase the pool of skilled labour?

---

52. (a) Why is stock control a very important part of a business?

   (b) Name and briefly explain four issues regarding stock control which must be addressed by businesses.

53. (a) Why is quality important to a business?

   (b) Define the following terms, showing the differences between them:
      (i) quality control
      (ii) quality assurance
      (iii) total quality management.

   (c) (i) What is meant by just-in-time manufacturing techniques?
      (ii) Give one advantage of using just-in-time manufacturing techniques.
      (iii) Give one disadvantage of using just-in-time manufacturing techniques.

3.5 WHAT ARE THE CHALLENGES FACING BUSINESSES?

54. (a) Descriptions of limited resources are given below. Match the descriptions A–D with the terms 1–4 by putting the appropriate numbers under each letter in the box below. Copy out the box first. Use each term only **once**.

Descriptions	Terms
A Computer experts and engineers	1 Specialist equipment
B Kidney dialysis machine for a hospital	2 Skilled labour
C Four-year fixed-rate bank loan	3 Land
D City-centre site for a department store	4 Finance

A	B	C	D

   (b) Wages for scarce resources such as computer experts are likely to be high. Explain why this is the case.

54. (c) Look again at descriptions A–D in part (a). Which **factor of production** does each description represent?

Copy and complete the following table. Factors of production can be used more than once.

Description	Factor of production
A Computer experts and engineers	
B Kidney dialysis machine	
C Four-year fixed-term bank loan	
D City-centre site for a department store	

55. Popudrinks Ltd is a large soft drinks manufacturer. The factory, although working at full capacity, is becoming run-down. Falling plaster injured a worker recently and faulty equipment nearly caused another accident shortly afterwards. Employees are becoming worried and restless.

   (a) Describe three types of staff responses which might soon occur if these problems are not resolved.

   (b) (i) Why do you think the management of Popudrinks Ltd have been reluctant to make the necessary improvements?
   (ii) Why do you think these improvements **are** necessary?

   (c) There are two main types of pressures faced by businesses – internal and external. Which **one** of these terms describes the pressures faced by Popudrinks Ltd?

56. A large construction business has won the contract to build an eight-lane motorway through attractive countryside. The project will take four years to build and will pass near some villages and a town.

   (a) Describe the internal pressures which the business might face.

   (b) The business will also face external pressures such as **political** involvement. List another three external issues which the business might face and give one example of each.

4 HOW ARE BUSINESSES MANAGED?

4.1 WHAT ARE THE KEY DECISIONS THAT BUSINESSES MAKE?

57. The following table lists four key questions which must be answered by the management of businesses.

Key Questions	Factors To Be Considered
What products will be made?	
What will the price be?	
Who will be employed?	
Where will the products be made?	

Copy the table. For **each** question, write in **one** factor which will be considered by management before making each decision.

58. Market research is now seen as an important tool for managers. After management decides to use market research, what three choices regarding market research are they then likely to make?

59. Managers also have to decide what combination of machines and people they want to employ. Describe three factors which will influence their decision.

60. Name three factors which must be considered when a business is deciding whether or not to expand its operations.

61.  Jonas Adjako, who lives in Glasgow, has built a prototype of a clockwork television. He hopes to produce and sell the televisions in countries where electricity is scarce and batteries are expensive.

    (a) Explain what is meant by a prototype.

    (b) Give two reasons why Jonas only has a prototype at present and has not gone into full production.

    (c) If Jonas decides to test the market for the product in Africa, how could he do this and what questions should he ask?

---

61. (d) After five years, Jonas has established a very successful market in various African countries. He now wants to market the clockwork televisions in Britain.
    (i) Name three ways in which the UK market will be different from the African market.
    (ii) Despite the differences referred to in part (i), give two reasons why some people might purchase this product in Britain.

    (e) Jonas has now established the **product** and the **place** of production. These are two elements of the marketing mix.
    (i) What are the other two elements of the marketing mix?
    (ii) How could Jonas use the other two elements to help him break into the UK market?

62.

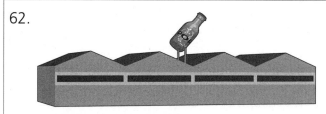 

This very large bottling plant uses a highly computerised and mechanised production line. There are only five members of staff employed to supervise the technology.

Bill Dyson, the owner of this shop, employs twenty paper-boys and paper-girls to deliver his newspapers each day. He works in the shop alone. His only equipment is a cash register and a small freezer for ice cream.

These two businesses use factors of production in very different combinations.

(a) Explain what is meant by this statement, showing clearly the ways in which these two businesses make different uses of the factors of production.

(b) Give reasons for these differences.

63.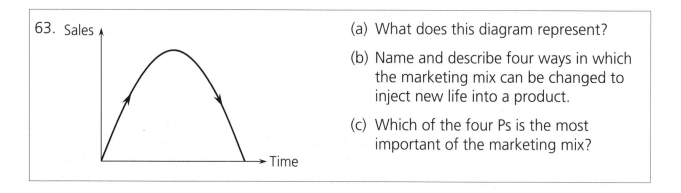

(a) What does this diagram represent?

(b) Name and describe four ways in which the marketing mix can be changed to inject new life into a product.

(c) Which of the four Ps is the most important of the marketing mix?

64. **Branding**, **image** and **packaging** are important parts of marketing.

Explain the three **bold** terms and state why they are important. Give examples where possible.

4.2 WHAT INFLUENCES THE DECISIONS?

65. (a) The management of a large car manufacturing company decides to produce a new model of car. They must first consider:

(i) the customers' needs   (ii) their own needs   (iii) competition from other businesses.

Copy and complete the following table by **listing** what you think the needs of each group will be. Two examples have been completed for you.

Customers' needs	Manufacturer's needs	Competition from other businesses
	low costs	cheaper prices

(b) The manufacturer must also consider social and legal issues.
Give two examples of social issues and two examples of legal issues which the manufacturer must consider.

(c) (i) Name two economic factors affecting customers' buying power.
(ii) Clearly explain how these economic factors will affect the car manufacturer's decision about what type of car to make.
(iii) How can an economic and political decision such as putting toll charges on British motorways affect the type of car which a business decides to make?

66. Zigzag Trading Company employs thirty workers. It advertises for a secretary to the Sales Manager. The three applicants pictured below are short-listed. The three candidates have similar academic qualifications and work experience. The management must treat the three applicants fairly, and employ one of them on merit. By law, there must be no unfair discrimination.

Sankha Nahar   Frances O'Neill   Roy Mearns

(a) Describe three examples of legislation which the management of Zigzag Trading Company must remember when considering the three applicants.

(b) The successful candidate is given a Contract of Employment to sign. Why do you think the management asked for this to be done?

66. (c) Zigzag Trading Company produces brightly
coloured clothes for children.

The Production Manager finds that when
test washing this new product, colours run
at 40°C. He decides the product cannot yet
be sold to the public legally.

What do you think influenced this decision?

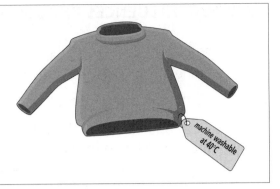

4.3 WHAT AIDS DECISION-MAKING?

67.

KiddiePix Ltd is a small business specialising in children's portrait photography. It is
responsible for the product from the photography to the framing of the picture.

(a) Sales targets have not been met. Which source of information in Mary Birst's office
shows this?

---

67. (b) Mary has decided that, as a result of sales targets not being met, she must replace one of her sales staff.
   (i) State which one you think she will choose, and why.
   (ii) What information source do you think she would base her decision on?

(c) External information has encouraged Mary to think that business will greatly improve very soon.
   (i) Name two external sources of information which are shown in the picture.
   (ii) State what information is contained in each source given in part (i) and state why they have made Mary more optimistic about business.

(d)

MEMORANDUM

To: Mary
From: James
Subject: Full-time assistant

We are in danger of losing customers.
A backlog of work has occurred due to a lack of staff. We need another photographer immediately.

Mary receives this memo from her photographer, James Grant.
   (i) State whether the memo is an example of internal or external information.
   (ii) Do you think Mary should consider employing another photographer soon?
   (iii) State which information sources, shown in the picture, helped you to make your decision in (d) (ii) and say why.

4.4 HOW ARE DECISIONS MADE?

68. Different management styles are shown in the following pictures.

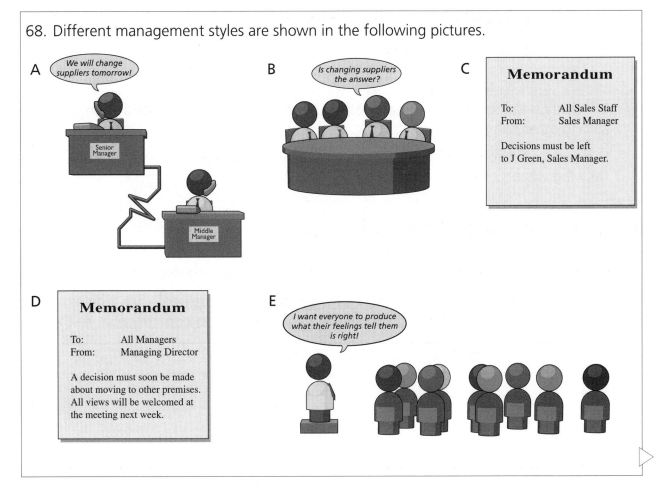

68. (a) Copy and complete the following table, by ticking the appropriate column for each picture. Use only **one** tick per picture. Management styles can be used more than once.

Picture	Type of management style		
	Democratic	Autocratic	Laissez-faire
A			
B			
C			
D			
E			

(b) (i) State one way in which a democratic management style can help motivate staff.
   (ii) How might an autocratic management style demotivate some staff?
   (iii) In which two of the following businesses do you think a laissez-faire style would probably work well?

   advertising   car manufacturing   dress design

   supermarket   oil production

   Give a reason for your answer.

69. Effective management involves **controlling**, **leading**, **planning** and **budgeting**, among other things.

   Use each of the four **bold** terms as headings. Write a paragraph on each of them, showing what each of these management roles involves.

4.5 HOW DO BUSINESSES COMMUNICATE?

70. (a) What is the main reason for businesses communicating with the outside world?

   (b) Copy and complete the following table, giving three examples of each type of communication which would be used by a Business Studies department in a school.

	Written	Spoken	IT
1			
2			
3			

70. (c) The following pictures show three different types of communication. Match the pictures with the descriptions below by completing the box.

Types of communication

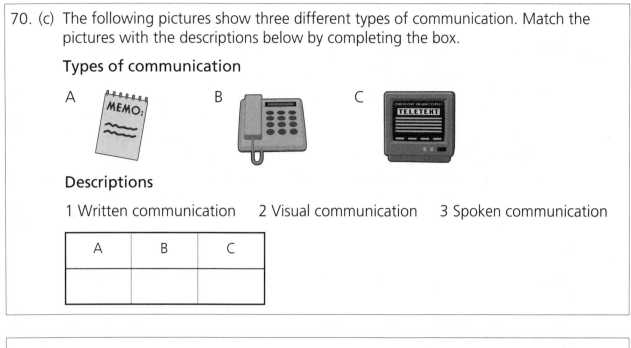

A   B   C

Descriptions

1 Written communication   2 Visual communication   3 Spoken communication

A	B	C

71. (a) Give three examples of **written** communication which might be used by a football club.

(b) Give two examples of occasions when a football club would convey information through the **spoken** word.

(c) What do the letters 'IT' stand for?

(d) Name two methods of IT which you could use to find out more about your local football club.

72. John Endersley, Production Manager, has a hard copy of a fifty-page report, the original of which is on disk. He also has the disk. He is based in Glasgow but wants to send the report to London.

(a) List four ways in which the report could be sent to London.

(b) Once the report arrives in London, it will be edited and sent back to John for final production. Which one of the four methods of communication listed in part (a) do you think would be the best in this case? Give reasons for your answer, showing that you have compared and evaluated each method.

73. Shirley Burns must send a memo from her branch in Liverpool to her Head Office in Edinburgh. The memo must reach Head Office in two hours' time.

(a) Is this an example of internal or external mail? Give a reason for your answer.

(b) There are two electronic methods of transmission which would be suitable for sending this memo. Name them.

(c) If a twenty-page article (which is currently on disk) is to be sent with the memo, which one of the two methods listed in part (b) would Shirley be advised **not** to choose? Give reasons for your answer.

74. (a) Why is clear communication important to the management of a company?

(b) Give three reasons why most managers now use information technology to help them communicate inside **and** outside their businesses.

75. (a) Copy and complete the following table, listing three methods of internal and external communication commonly used by an organisation.

Internal	External

(b) Selecting and using the appropriate IT is important in business. Match each form of IT listed below with its correct activity. The first one has been done for you.

Forms of IT

A Satellite link

B Word-processing

C Database

D Spreadsheet

E E-mail

Activities

1 Compiling a list of customers

2 Calculating wages

3 Sending a memo directly from one computer to another

4 Keying in and printing a report

5 A TV station in America sends a live broadcast to a TV station in the UK

A	B	C	D	E
5				